Variation in Living Things

Robert Snedden

Chicago, Illinois

www.capstonepub.com
Visit our website to find out more information about Heinemann-Raintree books.

To order:
☎ Phone 888-454-2279
💻 Visit www.capstonepub.com to browse our catalog and order online.

Edited by Andrew Farrow, Adrian Vigliano, and Diyan Leake
Designed by Victoria Allen
Picture research by Elizabeth Alexander
Illustrations by Oxford Designers & Illustrators
Originated by Capstone Global Library Ltd
Printed and bound in the United States by Corporate Graphics

15 14 13 12 11
10 9 8 7 6 5 4 3 2 1

Library of Congress Cataloging-in-Publication Data
Cataloging-in-Publication data is on file at the Library of Congress.

ISBN: 978-1-4109-4427-6 (HC) 978-1-4109-4434-4 (PB)

Acknowledgments
The author and publisher are grateful to the following for permission to reproduce copyright material: Corbis p. 27 (© Brian J. Skerry/National Geographic Society); Getty Images p. 41 (Evaristo SA/AFP); Moorfields communications team p. 39; Photolibrary pp. 5 (momentimages), 7 (Johann Schumacher), 10 (Javier Larrea), 13 (Dennis Kunkel), 28 (Gilles Martin), 29 (Bildagentur RM), 33 (Roger Eritja), 37 (Pixmann Limited), 40 (Gary K. Smith); Press Association Images p. 6 (Troy Maben); Science Photo Library p. 20 (Oak Ridge National Laboratory / U.S. Department Of Energy), 23 (Juergen Berger), 22 (Eye of Science), 38 (Philippe Plailly/ Eurelios; Shutterstock pp. 9 (© Mateusz Kopyt), 12 (© Katie Smith Photography), 17 (© Francois van Heerden), 14 (© Eduard Kyslynskyy), 19 top (© aguilarphoto), 19 bottom (© Denise Kappa), 21 (© HelleM), 24 (© r.nagy), 30 (© Malota), 34 (© Jan Hopgood), 35 (© FotoVeto), 36 (© Ron Hilton), 18 (© Linda Bucklin), 43 (© Valentyn Volkov), 43 (© Dulce Rubia), 43 (© Monticello), 42 (© Africa Studio), 42 (© Awardimages), 42 (© Zloneg), 42 (© matin), 43 (© Petr Malyshev), 43 (© Piotr Malczyk).

Cover photograph of blond (white) and brown grizzly bears playfighting reproduced with permission of Photolibrary (Steven Kazlowski/Peter Arnold Images).

Every effort has been made to contact copyright holders of material reproduced in this book. Any omissions will be rectified in subsequent printings if notice is given to the publisher.

Contents

Some words appear in the text in bold, **like this**. You can find out what they mean by looking in the glossary.

The Same–but Different

It is easy to see how some kinds of living thing are different. For example, a penguin looks very different from an owl. But how different can one penguin be from another, similar penguin?

Species

Scientists divide the living world into groups of similar living things. For example, birds are a group of animals that all have feathers. Birds can be divided up into smaller groups, such as penguins. The smallest division that can be made is the species, such as the king penguin. A species is a group of similar living things that have similar features, such as how they look. They are also able to **reproduce** (have young) with each other. Their young can also reproduce.

Variation

When living things come from the same **species** (see box above)—such as the king penguin—they look very similar. But there are still differences. The difference between members of the same species is called **variation**. For example, humans are a species of animal. You just have to look at the people around you to see how different humans can be.

This photo shows some of the rich variety among humans.

A Closer Look at Species

There is a lot of room for **variation** within a **species**.

The grolar bear

Grizzly bears are found in northern parts of North America. In recent years, they have moved into areas where polar bears roam. Polar bears and grizzly bears are closely related. But they are separate species.

Some polar bears and grizzly bears have **mated** (come together to have young). As a result, in 2006 the first "grolar bear" was found. It is the **offspring** (young) of a male grizzly bear and a female polar bear. The grolar bear is not a new species. It is a **hybrid**. A hybrid is a combination of two different species.

This grolar bear had a polar bear mother and a grizzly bear father.

Subspecies

The northern flicker is a species of woodpecker found in North America. There are two types of northern flicker from different areas. One has yellow wing feathers. The other has red wing feathers. When they meet, the two types easily mate. They produce young with mixed red and yellow feathers.

All of these birds are from the same species. But the different-colored woodpeckers are called **subspecies**. These are smaller groups within the same species.

This is the type of northern flicker with yellow wing feathers.

WORD BANK
hybrid   living thing that is the offspring (young) of parents from two
    different species
subspecies   smaller group within a species

7

Continuous variation

Within a **species**, there are two kinds of **variation**. For most features, members of a species show a wide range of differences. This is known as **continuous variation**. Height is an example of continuous variation. If you measured your class at school, for example, there will be a wide range of heights. This would range from the shortest to the tallest, with lots of heights in between.

The bell curve

If you were to measure everyone in a typical group and plot their heights on a graph, you would get a "bell-shaped curve" (see below). This shows how variations are spread out in a normal group. There is variation. But most people fall somewhere in the middle.

Number of people

Height

Discontinuous variation

For some types of variation, there are only a few separate possibilities for each feature. This is called **discontinuous variation**. One obvious example of this is **gender** (being male or female). Another is blood groups (see pages 30 and 31).

(see pages 30 and 31)

Can you roll your tongue? This is an example of discontinuous variation. People either can or cannot.

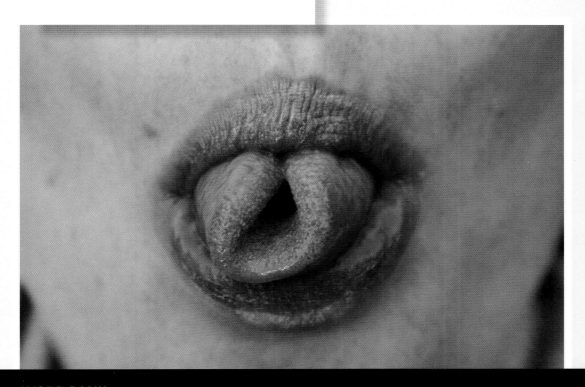

Common confusions

Eye color—continuous or discontinuous?

Sometimes eye color is described as a discontinuous variation. This is because people think of eyes as being brown, blue, or green. But eye color can range from almost black to very pale blue, with much variety in between. So, eye color is an example of continuous variation.

WORD BANK

continuous variation variation that takes place over a range of measurements—for example, height

discontinuous variation variation in which there are only a few separate varieties, with nothing in between—for example, gender

Generation to Generation

Living things always develop in a similar way to the parents that made them. For example, a pig will never give birth to a puppy. But why is this true?

Cells and genes

All living things start as a single **cell**. Cells are the smallest units of life. The cell keeps dividing until it becomes a fully formed living thing.

Each cell contains the information needed to perform this process. This information is stored in the cell as **genes**. Genes are instructions for the different **characteristics** (features) that each living thing has. They decide things like eye color or if someone will get a disease.

WHAT IT MEANS FOR US

It is useful for scientists to understand how genes work. In farming, scientists can try to understand why some crops might fight off disease or produce a lot of fruit.

Patterns of inheritance

Heredity is the process that passes features from parents to their young. It is why a pig gives birth to a pig. But how does it work?

A man named Gregor Mendel first studied heredity in pea plants. He learned that each characteristic—such as flower color—was determined by a separate unit. We now know to call them genes. The genes were found in pairs. One gene in a pair was **inherited**, or passed down from, the mother. The other gene was inherited from the father (see the artwork below). (For more on how this works, see pages 14 and 15.)

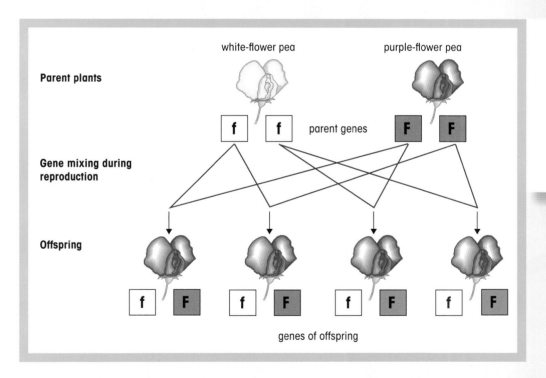

Parent plants

white-flower pea

purple-flower pea

| f | f | parent genes | F | F |

Gene mixing during reproduction

Offspring

| f | F | | f | F | | f | F | | f | F |

genes of offspring

These plants get one gene from each parent to determine their flower color.

Genetic variation

Each new living thing will have features in common with both its parents. This is because it has **genes** from each of them. Yet the new living thing will not be an exact match of either parent. Rather, it has a new combination of genes from both parents. This recombining of genes creates **variation** in a **species**.

Common confusions

Are identical twins really identical?

Do identical twins have the same genes? Not quite. There are some differences. These can be important. For example, one twin might develop a disease like cancer, while the other one does not.

Genome

All of the information needed to build a living thing and keep it alive is carried as instruction in its genes. The complete set of genes carried by a living thing is called its **genome**. Each member of a species has a very similar genome.

For example, the human genome makes all humans. From one person to the next, 99.9 percent of the human genome is exactly the same. It is just that 0.1 percent that makes us all different individuals. It explains how we look. It can also explain why we get an **inherited** disease.

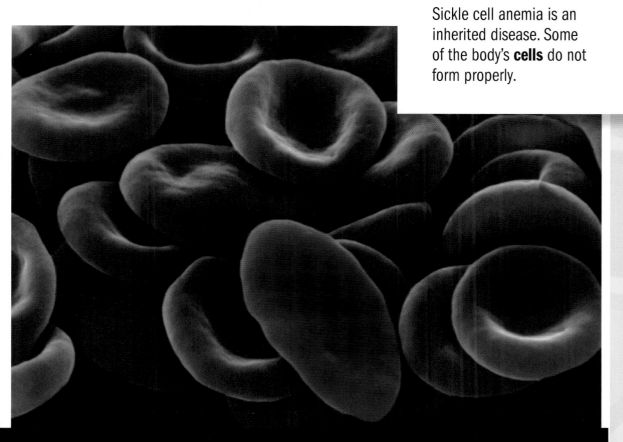

Sickle cell anemia is an inherited disease. Some of the body's **cells** do not form properly.

WORD BANK

genome information needed to build a living thing and keep it alive. Each member of a species has a very similar genome.

inherit process by which characteristics are passed from one generation to

Alleles

Look back at Mendel's pea plant experiment on page 11. One "parent" plant had purple flowers. The other "parent" plant had white flowers. Mendel **crossbred** the two types. This means he brought them together to have **offspring**.

For each feature—such as flower color—the offspring got two different forms of a **gene**. One came from each parent. These are called **alleles**. In the white parent plant, the alleles for flower color were both for white (f). In the purple parent plant, they were both for purple (F). When the two plants were crossed, the offspring got one purple allele and one white allele (fF). Yet the offspring were all purple. Why was this true?

The unusual coloring of a white tiger is caused by a recessive allele.

In the gene pair, the allele for purple flowers is **dominant** over the allele for white flowers. A dominant allele decides what **characteristic** is shown. The white flower allele is **recessive**. The characteristic of a recessive allele will always be hidden by a dominant allele. The characteristics of recessive alleles only show up when they make up both parts of a gene pair. For example, white flowers only appear in plants that have two white alleles.

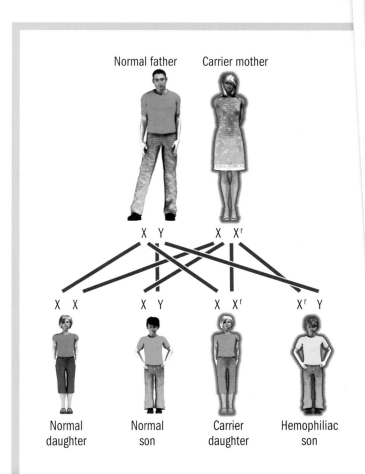

Normal father

Carrier mother

X Y

X Xʳ

X X

X Y

X Xʳ

Xʳ Y

Normal daughter

Normal son

Carrier daughter

Hemophiliac son

WHAT IT MEANS FOR US

Hemophilia is an **inherited** disease. It causes the blood to not clot (form a clump to stop bleeding) well. How is it inherited? Everyone inherits **genetic** material called **sex chromosomes**. Two X chromosomes (XX) make a female. An XY combination makes a male. The recessive gene that causes hemophilia is carried on the X chromosome (Xʳ in the diagram).

If boys inherit the faulty gene, they develop hemophilia. This is because they have only one X chromosome. They only have one allele for this trait, so even a recessive allele shows up. But girls have two X chromosomes. This means they have two alleles for the gene that causes hemophilia. If they get the faulty gene, they usually have a dominant, normal allele on their other "X" chromosome. The dominant allele masks the recessive gene. Still, they carry the disease. They can pass it on to their sons.

Multiplying differences

At first, Mendel was looking at single **characteristics** in his pea plants, such as flower color. Then, he began to look at more characteristics. For example, what if he **crossbred** tall plants that had purple flowers with short plants that had white flowers?

To understand what Mendel discovered, let's look at a diagram (see below). Let's say **gene** A controls height. Gene B controls flower color. Capital letters are used to show **dominant alleles** (tall and purple). Lowercase letters show **recessive alleles** (short and white). The blue boxes at the top show all the combinations of color and height one parent can have. The pink boxes on the left side list these same options for a second parent. In the middle are the 16 possible combinations.

Crossing two characteristics

Key

- alleles from parent 1
- alleles from parent 2
- tall with purple flowers
- tall with white flowers
- short with purple flowers
- short with white flowers

	AB	Ab	aB	ab
AB	AABB	AABb	AaBB	AaBb
Ab	AABb	AAbb	AaBb	AAbb
aB	AaBB	AaBb	aaBB	aaBb
ab	AaBb	AAbb	aaBb	aabb

But, of course, people have more than two characteristics. There are around 20,000 genes in the human **genome**! This creates endless possibilities for **variation** in humans.

Here we see the variety that just two genes can bring. The B gene determines eye color (B=brown eyes; b= blue eyes). The Y gene determines either curly hair (Y) or straight hair (y).

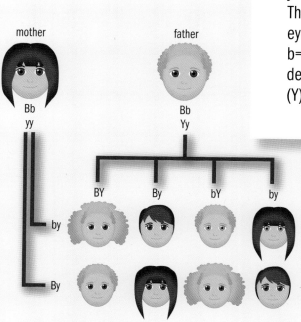

Cheetahs show very little variation. Cheetahs today are thought to come from a small number of relatives from long ago.

Variation and Environment

Genes play a major role in deciding how a living thing looks. But the **environment** (a living thing's surroundings) has a part to play, too.

Genotype and phenotype

The **genotype** is the complete set of instructions (genes) for an individual living thing. When these instructions are followed, we get the **phenotype**. The phenotype is the way a living thing looks.

A living thing's surroundings can affect how its appearance (phenotype) follows its instructions (genotype). For example, a living thing can have instructions to make a tall plant. But if there is a shortage of water in the soil, the plant will not grow as tall as it should.

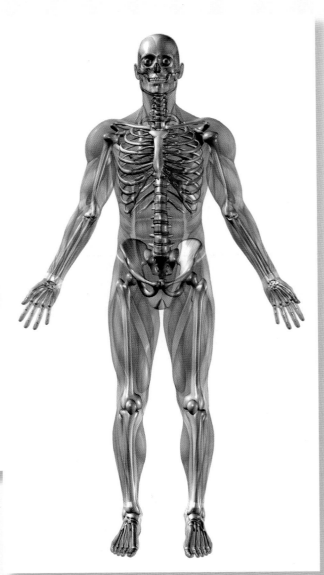

The way your body develops depends on outside factors, such as the amount of exercise you get.

Changing colors

The hydrangea is a popular garden shrub. The color of the flowers depends on how much of a substance called acid is present in the soil. The flowers can range from blue to pale purple to pink, depending on the amount of acid. So, the hydrangea's appearance (phenotype) is affected by its environment.

WORD BANK

genotype complete set of genetic instructions for an individual living thing

phenotype appearance of a living thing resulting from the interaction between

Genes and obesity

So, do **genes** or the **environment** decide how we are? For example, what determines **obesity** (being very overweight)?

So far, over 200 genes have been identified that are connected to body weight and fat. One of these is called the FTO gene. It is not found in everyone. But the people who have this gene are likely to be an average of 4½ to 6½ pounds (2 to 3 kilograms) heavier than those who do not. These people are more at risk for obesity.

Still, these people are not doomed to be overweight. They can make choices about their lifestyle (see page 21). This can work against the instructions from the genes.

The mouse on the left has a **mutation** in a gene (see page 22). This has caused it to gain more weight than the normal mouse on the right.

WHAT IT MEANS FOR US

A person's lifestyle, or environment, plays a big role in obesity. Many people have jobs that involve sitting at a desk all day. They might also choose unhealthy fast foods. This all leads to weight gain. But healthy lifestyle choices can change this. Eating the right foods and exercising regularly allow most people to control their weight. This is an important issue. Obesity can lead to serious problems such as heart disease.

This cat's weight is likely the result of too much food and too little exercise.

WORD BANK

obesity condition of being so overweight that health is endangered

Mutations

When a **cell** divides, its **genes** are copied (see page 10). Each new cell has a complete copy of the set of genes. But every once in a while, a mistake might be made during the copying process. When this happens, a gene will be produced that is different. These changed genes are called **mutations**. (Mutations can also sometimes be caused by harmful substances in the **environment**.)

Some mutations are not important enough to affect the living thing. But many mutations prevent the cell from functioning properly. As a result, the living thing may die.

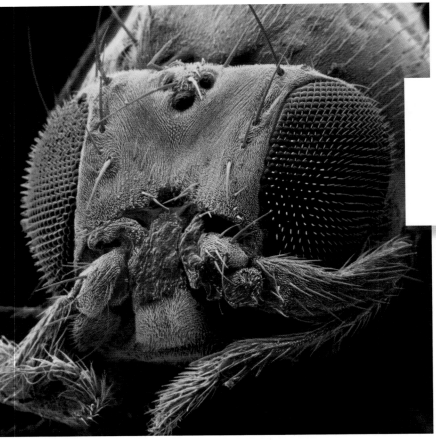

A mutation has made legs grow where this fruit fly's antennae should be.

Mutations and resistance

A few mutations can be of real benefit to a living thing. For example, some mutations can give insects the ability to resist the effects of **insecticides**. These are substances farmers use to kill insects. But mutations with resistances can create dangers for other living things (see box at right).

WHAT IT MEANS FOR US

MRSA is a type of **bacteria** (basic living thing). It can make people very sick. MRSA is very hard to treat. This is because it was the result of bacteria that formed a mutation. This mutation made them able to fight off the drugs (called **antibiotics**) used to treat illnesses caused by bacteria.

Tiny, round MRSA bacteria are shown here in yellow. They are clinging to fine hair-like structures inside the nose.

WORD BANK
mutation gene that has undergone change
insecticide substance used to kill insects

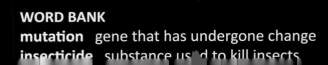

Variation and Evolution

Variations can help a **species** survive and develop.

Natural selection

We have seen how members of a species can have slightly different **genes**. These small variations might make them better at surviving in their **environment**. For example, they might have a special feature that makes it easy for them to get food.

Living things with these positive variations are the most likely to have young. They will pass their genes to their **offspring**. So, the offspring will be better able to survive in their environment, too. Meanwhile, individuals without the **characteristic** will die out. This entire process is called **natural selection**.

Scientist Charles Darwin first put forward the idea of natural selection.

Evolving species

Thanks to natural selection, a species **evolves**, or changes over time. The feature that allows it to survive keeps getting passed on to members of the species that survive. Over time, it becomes a common characteristic for the species overall.

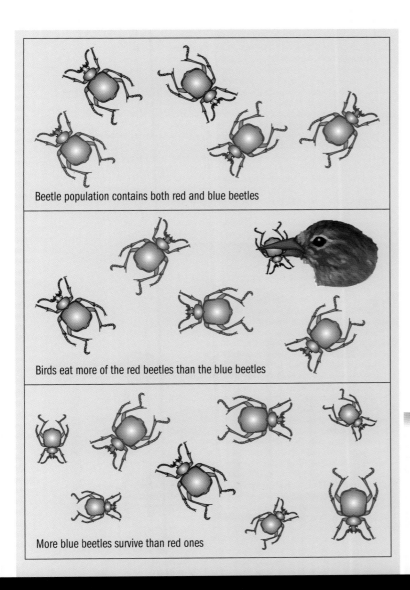

Beetle population contains both red and blue beetles

Birds eat more of the red beetles than the blue beetles

More blue beetles survive than red ones

This is a simple example of natural selection. There are two similar species of beetle—one red and one blue. Birds find red beetles tastier and easier to catch than blue beetles. So, over time, there will be many more blue beetles than red ones. Natural selection favors blue beetles.

Adaptations

An **adaptation** is a feature a living thing develops to survive. For example, thick fur is an adaptation that allows some animals to stay warm in cold parts of the world.

Scientist Charles Darwin learned a lot about adaptations. He traveled to the Galapagos Islands, in the Pacific Ocean. There he discovered several **species** of finch (a type of bird). They were all similar, but each had a particular adaptation. For example, one had a slender bill that was good for digging for insects. Another had a strong bill that was good for cracking seeds.

These adaptations allowed the finches to survive in different ways, eating different kinds of food. This meant that all the finches did not have to compete directly with each other to survive.

The Galapagos finch started out like the finch at the bottom. But the finches developed adaptations for different kinds of food. This led to all the different species found on the islands today.

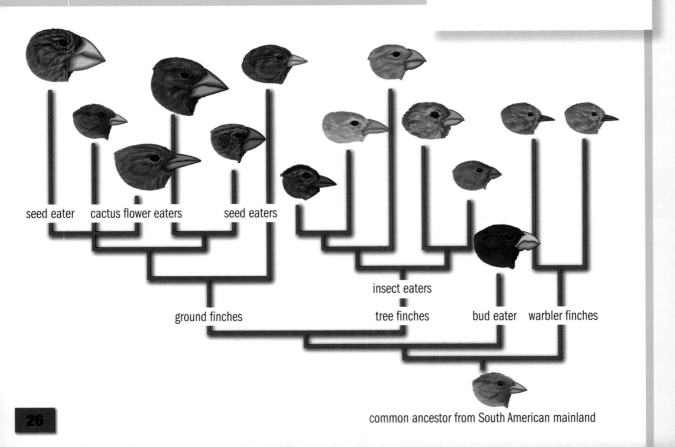

seed eater   cactus flower eaters   seed eaters

insect eaters

ground finches   tree finches   bud eater   warbler finches

common ancestor from South American mainland

New species

All of these different finches started out as a single species. But eventually the different types became so different that they no longer **bred** (came together to have young) with each other. They became new, separate species.

Newly hatched leatherback turtles have to reach the safety of the ocean. Otherwise, seabirds will eat them. Only the strongest will survive.

Cuckoo in the Nest

The common cuckoo of Europe does not build a nest of its own. Instead, it lays its eggs in the nests of other birds. The cuckoo lays an egg that looks like the host bird's eggs. That way, the egg can go unnoticed in the host's nest.

Each type of female cuckoo will only lay eggs that look like the eggs of a specific kind of bird. For example, a cuckoo that lays its eggs in a reed warbler's nest will only produce eggs that look like the reed warbler's eggs. This is a **discontinuous variation**. There are limited options for how a cuckoo's eggs will look.

The cuckoo's egg is larger than the reed warbler's. But the similar markings are enough to fool the reed warblers.

Survival tactics

When the cuckoo chick hatches, it pushes the host bird's eggs, or any chicks that have hatched, out of the nest. Once it has the nest to itself, it tricks its "parents" into feeding it. The cuckoo chick has a strange begging call. It sounds like a nest full of hungry chicks. The host birds respond to this by working hard to feed the cuckoo chick.

All of these tricks and **variations** have **evolved** over time. They have allowed the cuckoo to survive.

Catching the cuckoo

Some birds have evolved ways to catch the cuckoo. For example, the male reed warbler guards the nest when the female begins laying her eggs.

The cuckoo chick soon grows bigger than the reed warblers that feed it.

Blood Groups

Humans are divided into different blood groups. Many scientists believe that **variation** in human blood might provide defenses against some diseases.

The most common of the blood groups is called the ABO group. It can be divided into A, B, AB, and O blood types. The parts of the blood called **red blood cells** are different in each type. This is a type of **discontinuous variation**.

Blood bags are carefully labeled. Giving the wrong type of blood to someone could be disastrous.

The **rhesus (Rh) factor** is another part of blood groups. A person can be either type Rh positive or type Rh negative. (This refers to features on the red blood cells.) So, someone with blood type O who is Rh negative is called "O negative."

Blood transfusion

Hospitals keep supplies of blood. They use it for surgery or to replace blood lost by accident victims. The patient's blood type has to be discovered before receiving donated blood. If the wrong type of blood is given, the body will attack the new blood **cells** and destroy them.

This chart shows the different types of blood that can be given to patients (recipients). **Plasma** is the liquid that blood cells are found in.

Blood type of recipient	Donor		
	Blood	**Red blood cells**	**Plasma**
O+	O+ or O-	O+ or O-	O+, O-, A+, A-, B+, B-, AB+, or AB-
O-	O-	O-	O+, O-, A+, A-, B+, B-, AB+, or AB-
A+	A+ or A-	O+, O-, A+, or A-,	A+, A-, AB+, or AB-
A-	A-	A- or O-	A+, A-, AB+, or AB-
B+	B+ or B-	O+, O-, B+, or B-	B+, B-, AB+, or AB-
B-	B-	O- or B-	B+, B-, AB+, or AB-
AB+	AB+ or AB-	O+, O-, A+, A-, B+, B-, AB+, or AB-	AB+ or AB-
AB-	AB -	O-, A-, B-, or AB-,	AB+ or AB-

WHAT IT MEANS FOR US

People with type O blood can safely donate blood to anyone in the ABO group. However, they themselves can only receive type O blood. People who are AB can receive blood from people of any type.

WORD BANK
red blood cell type of blood cell that carries oxygen around the body in the blood
rhesus (Rh) factor feature of red blood cells that may be present in some people

Insect Societies

Some insects, such as ants, live together in large groups called **colonies**.

Roles in an ant colony

There are generally three types of insect within an ant colony. These are workers, queens, and males. The job of worker ants is to defend against attack. All of the worker ants are female and wingless.

Only the new queens and males can fly. They leave the colony to **mate** with ants from other colonies. After mating, the males die. He has finished his role. The queen lays her eggs. The eggs will one day form a new colony.

Genes or environment?

What decides whether an ant will become a queen or a worker? Researchers studied the Florida harvester ant. They found that the **offspring** of some males were more likely to become either queens or workers. This suggests **genes** are at play. They also noticed that young queen ants ate other animals. Meanwhile, young worker ants ate more plants. So, the **environment** plays a role, too.

Megacolony

Scientists recently discovered a huge "megacolony" of Argentine ants that stretches around the world. Originally from South America, the ants have been carried across the world by humans. One supercolony of ants is believed to extend 3,730 miles (6,000 kilometers) around the Mediterranean coast of Europe.

Worker ants walk with a winged male.

Artificial Variation

Throughout history, humans have tried to introduce **variations** into living things.

Artificial selection

Sometimes people **breed** plants or animals with a specific goal. They want to produce **offspring** with features that are useful. This is called **selective breeding**. For example, farmers want to have chickens that lay the most eggs. By breeding only from individuals that produce the most eggs, they will eventually have a new variety of the **species**. This new variety will be special in terms of how many eggs it lays. But it will not be a new species.

Farmers have grown many different varieties of pepper, from sweet bell peppers to hot chilies. All of them belong to the same species.

The gene pool

A **gene pool** is made up of all of the **genes** present within a species. By selectively breeding plants and animals to have certain **characteristics**, we are reducing the size of their gene pool. We are removing the features we don't want from the gene pool.

There are more than 300 varieties of pig, including this wild boar.

From wolf to dog

As many as 15,000 years ago, wolves became **domesticated**.
This means they were taught to live alongside people.
These domesticated wolves developed into the pet dogs
we know today.

The wolf in our homes

Scientists have proven that modern
dogs are closely related to wolves.
Researchers compared the **genomes**
of dogs and gray wolves. The difference
between the two is only 0.2 percent.

These wild wolves
are very closely
related to the dogs
that share many
of our homes.

Selective breeding in dogs

Most of today's dog varieties have been developed over the last 200 years. This had been done by **breeders**. These are people who carry out **selective breeding**. They work to produce dogs with certain **characteristics**.

The German shepherd dog is an example of selective breeding. At the end of the 1800s, Captain Max von Stephanitz **bred** mountain sheepdogs. He selected dogs that were strong and intelligent. That way, they could work as herding dogs. Herding dogs gather and lead animals such as sheep. The German shepherd became popular as a working dog for a number of activities, including police work.

All these dogs belong to the same **species**. Selective breeding has created large differences between them.

WORD BANK
domesticated   tamed to live alongside people
breeder   person who uses selective breeding to create plants or animals

Genetic engineering

Genetic engineering is when scientists change the **genes** of a living thing in a laboratory. They can take genes from one **species** and add them to another. What uses can this have?

Designer plants

Genetic engineering can make plants able to fight off powerful substances that are used to kill weeds. This helps farmers manage weeds—while not killing their crops in the process.

Another plant developed by genetic engineering is golden rice. A carrot gene was inserted into the rice plant. This made it produce more vitamin A. Many people in poor parts of the world lack vitamin A. So, this affordable rice can improve health.

This ram is being used to treat human diseases (see page 39).

WHAT IT MEANS FOR US

Cystic fibrosis is an **inherited** disease that attacks the lungs and digestive system (the body system that processes food). It is caused by a gene that doesn't work. This gene fails to produce a special substance called a **protein**. Scientists are using genetic engineering to help people with the disease. They insert a good copy of the gene into sheep. The sheep then produce the missing protein in their milk. This protein can be removed. It can be used to treat people with cystic fibrosis.

This doctor has learned to treat an inherited eye condition by using genetic engineering.

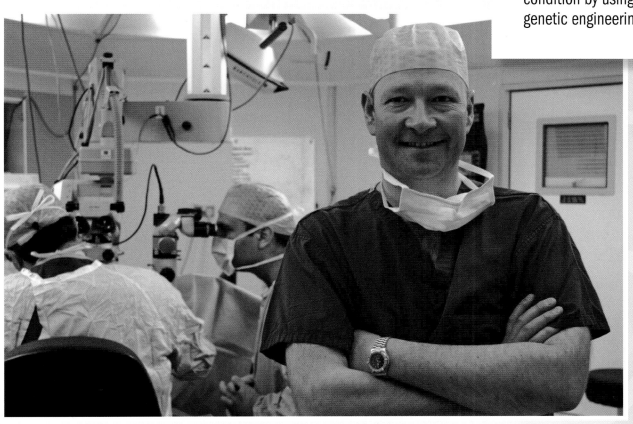

WORD BANK
genetic engineering changing the genes of a living thing in a laboratory
cystic fibrosis genetic disease that attacks the lungs and digestive system

Clones

A **clone** is a living things that has exactly the same **genes** as another living thing. There are many examples of clones in nature. Some strawberry plants grow from runners, rather than seeds (see the photo below). They have the exact same genes as the parent plant.

A strawberry plant spreads by producing offshoots called runners. The new plant is a clone.

Clone research

In 1997 researchers in Scotland cloned an animal. It was a sheep named Dolly. They took the **genetic** (gene-related) material from a sheep **cell**. They inserted it into an "empty" cell (with its genetic material removed). This new cell began dividing in the laboratory. Once it was growing, it was placed into a female sheep. It continued to develop inside her until it was ready to be born.

WHAT IT MEANS FOR US

Some people say the risks with cloned animals are worth it. For example, many animals could be **genetically engineered** to help treat **cystic fibrosis** (see page 39). This could save many lives.

The problems with cloning

Cloning animals is difficult and expensive. Over 90 percent of attempts fail. Many clones are unhealthy and die early.

Cloning and variation

Cloning also reduces the **variation** found in a **gene pool**. If a herd of clone animals were struck by disease, either all of them would live—or all of them would die. Without variation, they would all fight disease in the exact same way. This is a big risk.

The future probably holds a place for different kinds of cloning. But scientists must be careful about the risks.

This cow was the first cloned animal in Latin America. Her calf was born in September 2004. It is a normal calf, not a clone.

WORD BANK

clone living thing that has the exact same genes as another living thing

Food Variety

The fruits and vegetables we eat today have changed a lot from the ones eaten thousands of years ago. In the past, there was little variety. Since then, growers have produced a huge range of **variations** in food plants.

Potatoes

There are around 5,000 varieties of potato worldwide. About 3,000 of them are only found in the Andes Mountains, in South America.

Corn

Corn developed from something called teosinte. It had only five to twelve little kernels.

Kiwi fruit

The kiwi fruit was originally a hard berry that grew in China. Plant **breeders** in New Zealand developed the soft, green fruit eaten today.

Tomatoes

Tomatoes were once small, green fruits. Today, they can weigh 1,000 times more than early tomatoes! There are now thousands of varieties.

Cabbage

All the varieties of cabbage, Brussels sprouts, broccoli, and cauliflower we eat today developed from a wild cabbage.

Carrots

Carrots originally came in a wide variety of colors, including red, yellow, and even purple.

Wheat

Wheat, a type of grass, was first grown over 10,000 years ago. The first farmers selected varieties that had **mutations**. Large grains were firmly attached to the stalks. This led to the wheat we use today.

Eggplant

Many different varieties of eggplant are grown in parts of Asia. They can be reddish-purple, white, yellow, or green. They can be small and round or long and slim.

Apples

The first wild apples grew in Central Asia. Today, more than 7,500 varieties of apple are grown around the world.

Glossary

adaptation feature a living thing develops that makes it survive in its environment

allele one of a pair of different forms of a gene

antibiotic drug used to fight infections caused by bacteria

bacterium (more than one: **bacteria**) type of simple living thing

breed come together to have young

breeder person who uses selective breeding to create plants or animals with certain characteristics

cell basic unit of life

characteristic feature

clone living thing that has the exact same genes as another living thing. The word can also be used to describe the process of making the clone.

colony large group of insects, such as ants, that live and work together

continuous variation variation that takes place over a range of measurements—for example, height

crossbreed bring together different types of living things to create offspring (young)

cystic fibrosis genetic disease that attacks the lungs and digestive system

discontinuous variation variation in which there are only a few separate varieties, with nothing in between—for example, blood groups

domesticated tamed to live alongside people

dominant describes an allele that decides a characteristic of a living thing. For example, if a person has one hair color allele for brown hair and one for blonde hair, his or her hair will be brown. This is because the brown allele is dominant.

environment surroundings in which a living thing is found

evolve develop and change over time

gender being male or female

gene basic unit that passes characteristics from one generation to the next

gene pool all the variety of genes present within a species

genetic relating to genes

genetic engineering changing the genes of a living thing in a laboratory

genome information needed to build a living thing and keep it alive. Each member of a species has a very similar genome.

genotype complete set of genetic instructions for an individual living thing

hemophilia inherited disease in which the blood does not clot well

heredity transfer of characteristics from parents to their offspring (young)

hybrid living thing that is the offspring (young) of parents from two different species

inherit process by which characteristics are passed from one generation to the next

insecticide substance used to kill insects

mate come together to have young

MRSA (short for "Methicillin-resistant Staphylococcus aureus") dangerous bacteria that causes illness and is resistant to drugs like antibiotics

mutation gene that has undergone change

natural selection process by which individuals with a positive characteristic survive and reproduce, while living things without the characteristic die out

obesity condition of being so overweight that health is endangered

offspring young

phenotype appearance of a living thing resulting from the interaction between its genes and the environment

plasma liquid that blood cells are formed in

protein one of a group of complex substances produced by living things to perform tasks such as breaking down food and building cells

recessive describes an allele with characteristics that are masked when paired with a dominant allele. For example, if a person has one hair color allele for brown hair and one for blonde hair, his or her hair will be brown, because the blonde allele is recessive. A recessive allele's effects are only seen if both alleles in a gene pair are recessive (for example, the gene for blonde hair).

red blood cell type of blood cell that carries oxygen around the body in the blood

reproduce make offspring (young)

rhesus (Rh) factor feature of red blood cells that may be present in some people (rhesus positive) and not in others (rhesus negative)

selective breeding process of breeding plants or animals with the aim of producing offspring with the most useful features

sex chromosome genetic material that determines gender

species group of similar living things with shared features that are able to have young with each other

subspecies smaller group within a species

variation differences between members of the same species

Find Out More

Books

Bright, Michael. *The Diversity of Species* (Timeline: Life on Earth). Chicago: Heinemann Library, 2009.

Crosby, Jeff, and Sherly Ann Jackson. *Little Lions, Bull Baiters, and Hunting Hounds: A History of Dog Breeds.* Toronto: Tundra, 2008.

Farndon, John. *From DNA to GM Wheat* (Chain Reactions). Chicago: Heinemann Library, 2006.

Rand, Casey. *DNA and Heredity* (Investigating Cells). Chicago: Heinemann Library, 2011.

Vaughan, Jenny. *Genetics* (Science in the News). North Mankato, Minn.: Smart Apple Media, 2010.

Winston, Robert. *Evolution Revolution.* New York: Dorling Kindersley, 2009.

Wood, A. J. *Charles Darwin and the Beagle Adventure.* Cambridge, Mass.: Templar, 2009.

Websites

http://learn.genetics.utah.edu
Learn Genetics is a wonderfully detailed and comprehensive site with information on genes, heredity, variation, how cells work, and much more.

http://evolution.berkeley.edu/evolibrary/home.php
Understanding Evolution offers an excellent summary of ideas on how evolution works.

http://e360.yale.edu/feature/arctic_roamers_the_move_ of_southern_species_into_far_north/2370
This website has information about grolar bears and other hybrids.

http://web.pdx.edu/~cruzan/Kid%27s%20Mendel%20 Web/index.html
Find out about Gregor Mendel and his discoveries.

www.aboutdarwin.com
Learn more about the life and work of scientists Charles Darwin.

Topics to research

Dinovariation
What do we know about variation in living things that lived a long time ago, such as the dinosaurs? Did natural selection and adaptation work on dinosaurs and other prehistoric living things?

Here are a couple of places you could start looking for answers:

http://paleobiology.si.edu/dinosaurs/index.html

www.mnh.si.edu/exhibits/darwin/carrano.html

Classroom characteristics
How many different ways can you think of that the people in your class show variations compared to each other?

Index